POISON PEN LETTERS TO MYSELF

Romany is a compassi  wisdom extends far, far beyond l ɔf all who have shed tears for the ᴛᴏ1ᴇ7ᴇ15 1 in hope of that better tomorrow ... ᴛ...₅ ıₛ a guide of immense power and love that we may all be more thoughtful and aware of what lies behind seemingly random or unfair events that in fact are our greatest teachers.

Cassandra Eason, Author of *The Magick of Faeries* and *The New Crystal Bible*

Romany's poetry is personal and provocative. It is at times both brutal and beautiful, and this book takes the reader on a winding emotional journey. Despite the private and personal nature of much of her work, these poems do not exclude the reader – instead her style of writing allows you in, lets you walk within her words and interpret them in ways which are relevant to your own life.

Arietta Bryant, Author of *Ramblings & Rhymes* and *Circles of Sacred Laughter*

This anthology of poetry reads like a fragmented autobiography, stitched back together by a skilled hand to create a story of life, love and faith. Standalone poems speak simple truths; the collective speaks a wider story of becoming. Well written, these words tell a tale, give a lesson & speak to their reader through the simple words and the more complex intonation of phrase. A journey is had, through the poet's eyes; for the reader, the writer and the players involved; it reads like a novelised, journalised roadmap of the human experience. Even for the non-poet, this anthology is well worth a read – one can speed through it; half reading, half experiencing; or savour each poem alone. Either way, it is written with such fervour, time seems to stand still while the words leave their mark.

C.M. Mitchell, Author of the upcoming *Oakwood Collection* of novels

A self-effacing, insightful and wonderfully authentic document of a poet discovering her voice. Anyone who has ever taken a good look at themselves will find something here that speaks to them – there is honesty, catharsis and ultimately beauty on almost every page.

Laurie Goulding, Editor of *Mark of Calth* and *Gotrek & Felix: Lost Tales*

Poison Pen Letters is a consuming and compelling collection of raw expression. Within its pages we are drawn into a world of uncomfortable truths about both ourselves and the society we live in; the author addresses a number of topics which as individuals, we often choose to avoid. It was not difficult to find myself identifying with the text, which depicts the journey of an individual who has struggled through some of life's most difficult challenges and has found herself enlivened and empowered by her beliefs and the relationships made along the way.

There are also some further hidden meanings within the text – which will be evident to those who follow the same spiritual path – and wonderful motivational poems near the end of the manuscript, which give credence to the undeniable power of belief.

Vikki Bramshaw, Author of *Craft of the Wise* and *Dionysos: Exciter to Frenzy*

Poison Pen Letters to Myself

Poison Pen Letters
to Myself

Romany Rivers

MOON
BOOKS

Winchester, UK
Washington, USA

First published by Moon Books, 2014
Moon Books is an imprint of John Hunt Publishing Ltd., Laurel House, Station Approach,
Alresford, Hants, SO24 9JH, UK
office1@jhpbooks.net
www.johnhuntpublishing.com
www.moon-books.net

For distributor details and how to order please visit the 'Ordering' section on our website.

Text copyright: Romany Rivers 2013

ISBN: 978 1 78279 520 9

A CIP catalogue record for this book is available from the British Library.

Design: Lee Nash

Printed in the USA by Edwards Brothers Malloy

We operate a distinctive and ethical publishing philosophy in all
areas of our business, from our global network of authors to
production and worldwide distribution.

CONTENTS

Acknowledgements

I believe that it is always important to say thank you, so this is my simple note of gratitude. Thank you to everyone who touched my life, inspired my mind, and walked my path with me. Be our encounter creative or destructive, those moments have made me the woman I am today. Without you all, I would not be.

To my Husband; for promising on our wedding day and every day since to believe in me even when I doubt myself.

To my Son and Daughter; yes, your Mama really was young and foolish once upon a time. No, that does not mean you can make the same mistakes – go and make your own.

To my spiritual sister Arietta; for the tea, and for the sympathy, and for challenging me…

Introduction

The words in these pages were not written for mass consumption. They were not artfully crafted for reading aloud in dim rooms to a soundtrack of clicking fingers and Parisian style applause. They were not intended as political statements or a way of reaching other wayward wandering souls. Over the last two decades they were poured, purged, scribbled and spat onto scraps of paper, napkins, backs of hands, into empty pages and blank spaces of other books. At times of sorrow, frustration, confusion, acceptance and joy the words made sense of the mind's muddled meanderings. I make no apologies for the words that appear here. They are true to me, as simple and as intrinsic as the blood in my veins, the marrow in my bones.

Feast upon them at your leisure. Devour them, spit them out, dip in and taste them on your tongue. Be they bitter or sweet to you; know only that they have certainly improved with age.

Romany Rivers

Unexpected

The words came suddenly
In a rush
All at once
Like an unexpected orgasm
Surprising
Exciting
Relieving
Releasing
I did not realise just how dried up I had become
The river of emotion contained within
But you cannot contain a river without
Turning it into a dam
So
Was I damned?
No
I was paused
On a brink
Holding the potential
Before everything tipped and I
Became
   A
     Waterfall
Full of the kinetic
Unexpected

Red Letters

Trampled and trodden on, left lying on doormats. Tossed onto tables. Crumpled in coat pockets. Unceremoniously stuffed into the darkest recesses of overfilled handbags. Unopened. Unheeded. Most certainly unwanted. Not forgotten, but studiously ignored. The first one can be ignored, after all these things always come in threes. The third one, well, that one may be a problem. A little bit more serious. The first one? It is not really a warning, more of a nudge. A gentle reminder. There is no time, no resources, no need to worry about it right now.

If someone asks, deny everything. No responsibility. No liability. Plead ignorance. It never happened. You never got that warning. You didn't know there was a problem. Of course, yes, you really should be keeping a close eye on matters, but life is so busy.

Smile. Play make believe. Pretend there are no issues. Consciously ignore the warning. Subconsciously prepare your reasons, your excuses, your denials. If someone asks, get ready to fake it. Always be ready. Always a little on edge, a little defensive, a little ashamed that your inability to manage things has come to this. A red letter.

If someone asks, shrug it off. It is not a problem. It is something that can be dealt with later. Really, despite the evidence, you have it all under control. No need to worry. Everything is fine, just fine.

But no one asks.

No one notices.

No one really cares.

It is just one warning, just one red letter.

Before Bedtime

Sadness is a funny little thing
It sneaks around behind the sofa
And curls up in your lap when you relax
It gets heavier as the lights go down
Until you are afraid to move
Just in case it wakes up
Instead you let your legs grow numb
Your arms melt into your fingertips
Your head tips forward like a forgotten marionette
And you stay always
Curled around the pain of the weight held near the butterflies
Tomorrow you might open your eyes
But tonight is just fine……..

Home

Outside
Under the wide black starry skies
Barefoot
Weeping as my veins take root
This blackened town
Nothing nowhere
Rusted crown
Someone somewhere
Was I christened a someone
To no-one
In particular?

And it all comes down to fear
Fear that no-one really cares
If I fight to make my way out there
Or if I bleed to death standing here

Vale of Tears

I watched the shadows creep as I listened
And when you listened to me
I felt like I had finally spoken
The words washed me dry of tears
Emptied me
Black and hollow
It felt like a night of confession
A night of soul searching
We searched
But the soul I lost remains with you
My heart
Hollow without you
Nothing
But a vale of tears

What Have I Become?

What have I become?
A stale heart with luke-warm blood
Muddied knees and frozen tongue
Bloodless, tearless, blackened, numb.

Mirror, mirror, tell me lies
Say I'm young to the eye
For I am not to question why
Simply born to do and die.

Bitter

Windows like warm firelight
Draw my bitter curiosity in
And I stand in sullen emotion
Seeking every sin
I will take you home
And take you in
All in sullen emotion
All in sweet sin

Open the door for me
I lost the key
Open the windows then
Let the noise drift to me
See me standing
Too afraid to knock
Smiling on the outside
Laughing at the lock

I will take you home
If you lose yourself in me
And I will let you go
When I have what I need
Lose yourself in me for a while
Leave you with the image…
…of my smile.

If

If I fight hard enough
I don't need to fight
And if I learn enough
I don't need an opinion
If I shout loud enough
I don't need to be right
And if I fake an identity
I don't need to be anyone

I would bleed myself to sleep
and still never know
I would drown myself in books
and still never know
I would pick apart my scabs
and still never know
I would lose myself in smoke
and still never know

If I work hard enough
I don't need to work
And if I search everywhere
I don't need to seek
If I suffer for everyone
I don't need to suffer
But if I am just human
I am weak

I would stuff myself with food
and still never know
I would make myself so sick
and still never know

I would sink a bottle
and still not know
I would scream at the voices
and they still won't go...

...If I...

Our Millennium

They sit like little zombies
Eyes glazed with TV death
Their digitized heart beats
Their microwave breath
A wasted muscle flutters
Caught and woven into the web
A brief mental struggle
From one not assimilated yet
Technology spreads like fever
Children born with the bug
Unholy world wide communion
The new never new enough
Tomorrow's world yesterday
Armageddon come and gone
The living dead in unsocial society
This is our millennium

Smiling Again

On the outside looking in again
Smiling through my secret pain
What am I doing here
But wearing masks and facing fears
Longing for the past
Times that never last
Understanding more
Learning less
Never feeling of the rest

Smiling again…

Reaction learnt
No reason why
Only realised on goodbye

Smiling again…

Green upon Black

On days like these
I can only see
Green upon black
Hatred turns my cheek
So that I can't see
Behind me
The past at my back
I look ahead
To a future dead
I wish I were too
Though I am linked to this life
My blood in you
Peel my eyes from your beating heart
Feel the sharpness there
Pluck my fingers from your eyes
See my self abuse

I'm too tired to hate
Too fired up to be calm
Too angry to die
Too self piteous to harm
Too twisted up in emotion to see
Too trapped in my mind to ever be free
Too much
Too little
Too soon
Too late

I want to curl
In the womb of depression
I want to tear

My way out and destroy
But I
I
I am
So
So tired

So tired

Desert Tongue

Motherhood and mayhem
Please find the words to tell them
Desert on my tongue
Rain in my eyes

Brotherhood and bitches
Turning rags from riches
Dying for my truth
Living their lies

Simply biding my time
Riding out my crimes
Holding it all in, running blind
Howling at the night
Hiding from the white light
Keep calm
Carry on
Tow the line

Bleeding hands
Hold shattered dreams
Watching all the fractions gleam
Knowing they are pieces of my life
Now I wonder how long I can
Hold this nightmare in my hands
Without the effort weeping me dry

No, just leave me alone

Remote Suicide

It's been so long
I'm just sitting by
Watching him watch me
As he damages my life

I've tried to cope
Leaving him to rage and cry
Knowing that the truth to me
To him is an elaborate lie

I wonder why
He acts like the moth to my flame

Without A Trace

The world is crashing down
Tumbling years
So loud I cannot hear my screams
Torn from old dreams
Ripped from my very soul
Left as a gaping whole

Even though the end is near
I have no heart
Lost all my fears
The sea storms by me
A cesspool of tears
Boiling far and rushing near

The waves are red with blood
Hands dance towards the sky
I watch my life of destruction
With pure fascination
Now the end of my world is nigh

Infernal

I have a little problem
An infernal love
Torn me wide open
Under the biblical sun
Down you took me
Sad and lonely
Into your confused and confusing heart
Where you accepted
Smiled and respected
Talked, trusted and laughed
As wrong as this may be
I feel you have stolen a part of me
And even though we both feel sad and guilty
I don't think I want it back
Kiss me through your tears and mine
Kiss me through your pain
Kiss me heart, body and mind
Kiss me once again

Never mind

Wasted days and sleepless nights
Trapped a lonely soul in mid-flight
Joining peace with the holy slave
Whispering softly from the grave
Careless dreams, used illusions
Can't help drowning in such confusion
Frightened years, hopeless tears
Lost child moaning quiet fears

Abandoned hopes, unloved heart
Empty eyes facing unwanted dark
Harmless mind, sedated soul
Sinking in oceans black and cold
Broken mind, unlived dreams
Scars aren't always seen
Fractured life, unnoticed death
Always waiting for the dying breath

Needing love, never enough
Suffer the smooth, rejoice the rough
Unfeeling pain, pouring rain
Spinning around and around again
All set me free, leaving me
To feel feelings that I'll never be…
Unable to shout, no way out
Left facing a black shadow of doubt…

What does my life really mean to me?

Return To Sender

Occupying the same space as a previous self, unwilling to receive the words and wants of others. Intentionally or unintentionally returning all that is no longer wanted, needed or useful. Send it back where it belongs, wherever that is. Somewhere, out there, bouncing back and forth between recipients who refuse to recognise or take ownership. Somewhere, out there, its journey will stall in dusty store rooms, on overloaded shelves, or end its life rotting in a pile of discarded dreams.

This is not for you, not now, not ever again. Return it all with disinterest, spare it no thought, let it drift away like dust upon the breeze. Return it with indignation, with spit and scribble, with a swift crumple and crush in angry fist. Return it with understanding. Understand that once, maybe, this was something you needed, wanted, requested, desired, or asked for. Understand that it is not for you any longer. Understand that by sending it back you are saying more than no, you are saying I no longer recognise this need or the person that needed it.

Take as much or as little time as you need to gaze or glance at these windows of the past. Let your fingers run over the names and places. Let your mind wander down the avenues of nostalgia and reminiscence. Turn them over in your hands and take note of the return address. Maybe this too has changed, maybe they too have moved along. Perhaps they send this to you from a place you no longer recognise, somewhere out there, unfamiliar and uncomforting. Swiftly or slowly make that judgement call. This is not for you, not anymore, not ever again. With lightened heart and heavy pen, make that acknowledgment to the world. Send it back from whence it came.

Ever abide the law of three, for what ye gives out comes back to thee.

Keep Searching

I see you watching
Digging
For dirt
I know where you are coming from
I can see your future path clearer than you
A sense of superiority in my words
But why not
I worked hard for my vantage point
I climbed high
With bruised lips
Battered hips
Cracked joints
Bloodied knees
Scratched and scratching fingers
And eyes blurred with tears
And still I pushed
Pulled
Clambered
Climbed
You slither on your belly
What can you see from there?
You nip at everyone's ankles
A thorn in the Achilles
A stone in the shoe
But the pain that we have felt because of you
Is nothing in comparison to the bright white light of true rebirth
There is no price tag to learning the lessons of life
You cannot hold a hand in false support and sympathy
Whilst writing a bill with the other
You can be worth it -
But not in this incarnation

Moral Masquerade

What are you doing?
You are talking of killing
Murdering
Innocent people
Women and children
Sisters and daughters
Mothers
Lovers
Brothers
Fathers, husbands and wives
Children yet to live their lives
What are you doing?
Filling hearts and minds
With truth and lies
Of enemies
We cannot see
Those who would take my freedom from me
For taking freedoms from you
And yet I lift a hand to no one
Not to attack
Nor to defend
Not even to be counted amongst good men
What are you doing?
Raising hands
And sights
In long days and dark nights
What are you doing?
Creating a nation
Of militant self righteous rage
Of fear
Of hate

Of impossibility to relate
Of belief
Of morality, mortality
Of religious superiority
What are you doing?
Do you speak for me
Even when I raise a voice against you?
Do you represent the people
When the people march against you?
What are you doing?
Creating
Perpetuating
A battle of sacred rage
Are we really the people, the power and the change?
Or simply another moral masquerade?

Question

Sometimes it feels like I cannot win
I understand that this is not a competition
But if it is not,
Why does it always feel like a battle?

The Pulling

I stood under the not quite Moon
And looked up at the slightly obscured stars
I felt like I had been going nowhere
But I knew that I had come far
My feet were sore and my heart heavy
But the pulling still tugged at my belly
I followed my umbilical cord
Back to the beginning of never
I wondered if I would be reborn
Or would I be pulled forever
It occurred to me then
That I was
Paused

Maybe this is what they mean by choice

Primal Torture

There's nothing quite like
The sounds of primal torture
The tear of flesh
The eternal blood rush
Pushing
Just a little further
Into the unknown
Nothing feels as right
As the pain of primal torture
The slightly sexual thrill
The sight of ink and blood spill
Aching
Itching
For just a little more
Of what the flesh has yet to know
The boundaries breached
The heights reached
Of Shaking
Quaking
Rushing
Buzzing
Ecstasy
The dizzy spinning feeling
Achieved with every piercing
And every splash of colour
The tribal markings
Of our time at war
And those who don't believe
In that bitter sweet release
In the pride of our colour
In flesh fading never

In the blood let
The rush
The thrill
Then they are not of our clan
And they never will
Adore those screams of primal torture

Brandy for Brian

It scared me
When I first saw him
Dishevelled and desperate
I could not console him
But then why should I?
I didn't really know him
But I would mother his children
And I think he knows it
They were such long nights
Of strumming on the guitar
Sipping brandy with Brian
On the living room floor
And I fell so deep
That I still can't believe
Winter's chasing off those late summer evenings

Stitches

I have felt myself fall apart
And I have bled wept back together
I have felt and I have hurt
And I have known it was not forever
So strange to think you blind
To the scars I thought so clear
Can't take my easy smile
Just hear what you want to hear
I can't take this anymore
My eyes are dry
My throat is sore
This time I won't fall apart
My stitches hold when I laugh so hard
I guess you never knew me at all

You watch me in confusion
She watches me in anger
Still I smile at you
When you think that I should hate her
So strange to think you blind
In worry
Or in fear
When to me it is so clear
If she makes you so happy, who cares?

I can't take this bullshit anymore
See my eyes are dry
My throat red raw
For you I will not fall apart
When I watch you watch me I laugh so hard
It hurts

Inside
Didn't you take the time to know me at all?

Blind Eyes

Every word I say
Every move I make
Asleep or awake
Every choice I choose
Every path I tread
Followed or led
Won't go unnoticed
By unseen eyes
Wet or dry
Won't go unnoticed
By unseen ears
Far or near
Won't go unnoticed
By unseen lips
Spoken or silent
Won't go unnoticed
By unseen fists
To hold or hit
Those eyes strive
To watch and see
Everybody
Maybe too busy
To see
Little me?

The Freak

You breathe mystery
Hold as if embracing insecurity
Sense still a mask behind the make up
A treasure within guarded defensively
Watch and read
Your body speaks, your eyes speak
They bring forth the springtime wells
Yet conquer not the dry mouth desert heat

I am torn in two
To mother you
To heal you
To bold as brass
Sup your glass
Dry as bone
Serving mine own

Speak to me
Weep to me
Bleed to me
For we are weak when lonely
Dancing around a new emotion
Each as hunter
Each as prey
Stepping forward in armour
And dancing away

Fire in the dark hall
Be I moth to your flame
Read me, read my scars
Familiar with pain

Read me willing and unashamed
Look to me
Faint smile
Arms wide...

Prove Your Point (Carry On)

Don't play these games with me
You don't seem to realise
You can't push me, pull me
Make me cry and compromise
Don't try to control me
You just don't seem to understand
I won't beg
Bleed
Love
Or fear you
I will never take you by the hand
Love me
Love me not
I really don't care
Don't give a fuck
Want me
Want me not
We will stay in this awkward place
Until you have the guts to spit in my face
Hear me
Hear me not
I don't need you to make me be
I don't want you
You are nothing to me
You can vie for superiority
Because deep down you feel second best
You can keep trying to push me down
Just proves you are no better than the rest
Feel the need to put one over on me
Just shows your own stupidity
I will never change

I will always be
The one confirming your inferiority

Tribe

The fear of depravation
Is the result of the unknown
The freak who cries alone
The conformity of a nation
Is the result of constant selling
The underground now telling
Of a tribe ever rising
Reaching dizzy heights of difference
In a land of song and dance
The media forever lying
About members misunderstood
A bloody band
A cult
A hood
But bloody we stand together
Without guilt, fear or shame
Laughing with personalised pain
And rise we will forever
In new forms of frightening strangeness
Grinning at you from the darkness

Goodbye

Hold me through your tears and mine
Kiss me one more time
Split second choices, a lifetime long
When I wake it hurts to find you gone

Once Upon A Time...

I watched you as you walked in
I saw the love that you feel for me and I was annoyed
I don't know where your love comes from
A need to be loved
A need to own possess undress
I closed my eyes to shut out the prying fingers
The tentacles of concern close in
So tired now
Just want to sleep
Dream that I enjoy sex
Once upon a time
Dream that I enjoy touch, love, hugs
Once upon a time
I don't understand the crashing in my head
The lack of security in my bed
I adored the feeling of being
Once upon a time
I adored the needing, feeding, receiving
Once upon a time
Now I don't know if it's mine
Or just yours
You left me tea
And time to breathe
I wake up
Put on my make up
Paint on a smile over the sigh
And wonder about once upon a time

June

It was a terrible day
Of thunder and rain
The sunshine so far away
So I crept and crawled
To face all the things I did not want to say
And pulled my way
Into a smiling frame
Soon it felt unreal
And I hated my own untruth
But I found that the lie
Belied
The reality of unreality
And all the opportunities
That arise
I still smiled
And cringed
And listened to my own words of advice
Spoken from necessity
I heard myself
Reflected in another's eyes
I saw all they see
And realised why they need me
Not for my strengths
Nor my weaknesses
Not for my availability
Superiority
Or inferiority
Not even because I am simply me
Or that I am in bonds
Or wild and free
But because

When they look at me
And all I achieve
They see I am only human
With dreams made a reality
Something that they too can be

On Reflection

Give me the chance to be
Extraordinary
Give me the chance to be
More than the best that I can be
Give me the chance to leave my mark
On the lives and hearts of others
Give me the chance to be the name
That pauses on the lips of old lovers
Give me an opening
Something I can work on
Give me a focus
A push in the right direction
Give me a reason
An excuse to keep moving on
Give me a little hope
A glimmer in the dark to keep me warm
Give me a little faith
Just to help keep me sane
Give me something
So that I am no longer afraid

Ok, how about this?
Just give me a clear mirror
So that I can take a good long look
And see just who the hell I am

Addressee Unknown

Moving on, burning bridges and turning your back on old familiar haunts. Consciously saying goodbye and refusing to return. Walking with back straight, never once turning around lest the fear take hold and somehow you find yourself back where you started. Running now, before that little voice gains momentum and insists that your actions are unreasonable. Leaping and hurtling towards a future uncertain, without forwarding address, without knowledge of a safe haven nearby. Knowing only that in your heart, this is the right thing to do. Trusting that your feet will guide you to a place of peace.

Still, those around you do not understand. You wish to move away from the place they are still comfortable in. Voices of concern, of advice, of insistence fill your mind as you head towards distant shores. Perhaps you lie. Lie to everyone, including yourself. Perhaps you say that you will indeed send back a letter, a card, a greeting. Perhaps you say that you will indeed pass on a forwarding address when you know where you will be. Perhaps you will, for a select few. For those who love you enough to let you go. For those who understand your journey, your need to move past your past, your desire to find a sanctuary.

The honest truth is, you don't know where you will be, or whether you will ever reach your destination. Perhaps you never will find what you seek. Perhaps you will always be moving on, moving away, moving forward. In your wake you leave a memory that fades, disappears into the forever changing landscape until it is unrecognisable. Those left behind will hastily inscribed 'Addressee Unknown', and continue with their busy lives.

When you look back at the person who was, they will be unrecognisable to you also. That person no longer exists. Not here, not there, not anywhere. You too will hastily inscribe 'Addressee Unknown' and you too will go about your busy life, without more than passing thought of what once was.

Dedication

Born as Romany Rivers
Now I am,
And I feel there is no light in my life
But that which was there in the beginning
And will be there at the end
The Goddess guides us all
To walk her path
And this day I felt that I have long ago
Placed my feet upon her path
And yet have only walked it in my dreams
I have pledged myself to thee
Mother of all, and to you the Hunter,
The consort of love and laughter
And safe in this knowledge of re-awakening –
I am born all over again.

Universal Self

I have so much to achieve
For you, for them, for me
I feel old, young and ageless
But time keeps me running out
I move faster than the speed of light
So that I can be there and here
All at the same time
I think there must be more than one of me
I catch myself all the time
Looking the same but different somehow
And I surprise myself
Maybe that is why you all look so surprised
When occasionally
I am not to be found anywhere

Dear John

There was a man once
Who held me in his arms
Who touched me deep inside
Who smothered me in his insecurities
I held him in my heart
I felt him in my mind
I took him into me
Without him knowing
Who I was
Who I am
Who I will be
He made me feel at home
He made me want to run away
I stayed bound to his smile
Tied into his unnecessary jealousies
He felt without reason
Pulled me close without seeing
Touched without believing
I felt with intention
Pulled him close with understanding
Touched him with analysis
Knowing that
Every minute I embraced
His strangeness
His freshness
His anger
His laughter
I was creating a memory
That would ease my loneliness
In times to come

Fat Happy Pre-packaged Dreams

The paper bag danced with the breeze
Teasing taunting titillating
I heard someone say a curse for the mess of today
I left it to dance for minutes
Before I put it away
To rot within our mothers belly
A waste product of a mentality
Born when we stopped feeling hungry

I Pray

I walk the woodland paths
And know
I'll never be alone
I hear the whispering leaves
The subtle way they call me home
I feel the touch of earth
The ways its roots, they pull me in
Connects the universe
Forever in eternal spin

I pray that Mother Earth will turn each day

I hear the storm arrive
The whistling wind, it whips on by
It makes me feel alive
It gives me wings
It makes me fly
I hear the whispered words
Rushing past upon the breeze
A sense of wisdom heard
That lifts me up and sets me free

I pray the winds, they will forever change

And I will not take for granted
That which is there for me
No, I will not take for granted....

Scrying

Look into the blackened glass
See the images of time gone past
Watch the sorrow, feel the pain
Hear the laughter amidst the rain
From this past we must learn
For it relives now as the wheel turns
What was once will be again
Time gone the time has come
We must accept all our fears
What was done will not be undone
Our future is held loosely
By the hands of our young
They cannot see beyond our words
Tales of life woven and spun
I can see images of the future
Within the darkness before me
But they appear older than the lives
Of those that spawned me
What have we done?
What will we do?
The images fade without answers
It is up to me and you.

Destiny

The cards slip through my hands
I drift into the world of unreality
Of possibilities
Probabilities
But never inevitabilities

Sleep Deep

We welcome you and say farewell little one,
All within the same breath
We hold you in our hearts dear one,
Sense the presence you have left
For your journey with us was swift and brief
But your influence as long as memories
We hold each other within our grief
But understand it was not to be
No sounds of footsteps upon the floor
No sticky finger marks upon the walls
No toys embedded within sofa cushions
No gleeful giggles or worried calls
These childhood things are not the gifts you bring,
But you impart a gift like no other
From your very soul you have given a blessing
The chance to become a Father and a Mother

Your life on Earth been and gone
Now sleep deep little one

Lake of Unshed

You kissed away my tears and I was
Refreshed
I try to smile with you
But I think I always look confused
Bemused
Our lives are strange
Together in a separate fashion
Or are we separate but still together?
We talk about children of today and tomorrow
Our children
Or just hers and his and theirs and they will be soons?
I wonder if we can stay in this business partnership
Talking
Voting
Agreeing
Negotiating
When will we argue?
Purge?
Scream?
And run away?
Is that not how things are done today?
Are we Saints to be raised unto the heavens?
A light of inspiration for others?
Or are we just belying the truth?
Look at everyone around us
See in their eyes the ice blue of reflection
And yet I cannot see where we are
I see us in the middle ground of a painting
The mountains loom
Will we ever surpass them?
Or are we too tired from teamwork

Swimming
Across a lake of green
The lake of hard work
A good relationship
Time off together
Time away with friends
Shared interests and differing hobbies
A deep satisfying beautiful azure-green lake of time well spent
But I wonder
Truly
Is this not a lake of stored
Unshed
Tears?

Passing Through

Too many faces
Not enough names
Too many places
So many the same
Too much freedom
Not enough focus
Too many dreams
So many so hopeless

My life on my back
I carry my past with me
Feeling overexposed
But no one takes the time to see
Take me down
Take me in
All you see is my sore feet

Musings

Every time I see her
She makes me smile before I see her eyes
I cannot watch her dance without thinking of a thousand poetical
    words
They run through my mind
They pass too fast for my typing fingers
But remain linger and last
In ways I cannot explain
Her grace astounds me
Defying gravity
Silver fish in a rainbow river
She likes the
            Spaces
                Between
                    The
                        Words
As much as the language itself
And this teaches me something new always
Lessons gentle, salty and severe
She speaks with an Elvish tongue
That only the trees can hear
I catch the whispering amongst the branches
As they all talk about her in ages past
They will continue to discuss her
In lives yet realised
I think she reflects a part of me
Not yet discovered
Like a sandcastle in the mind
Fragile and grainy
Not yet created
Until the summer months

But I like autumn
I like the way she looks
Like the leaves changing
Red gold green honey
She looks like the cold snappy refreshing days that brighten your
    cheeks
Warm your heart and bring blood
Rushing in response
To the morning breeze
I feel my blood sluggish now
Speeding up
Rushing
Weaving
Knitting together in my veins to re-create my soul
I am always surprised how one person
Can make such a difference without action, words or conscious
    inspiration
This is just one of the ways she appears to me
A muse

Undine

Hold my hand
Please walk along beside me
I am a cardinal water spirit
Fast flowing free
Let me take you underground
Into the caverns of the soul
If you can stop the tide I will give you back
Old opportunities you let go
I am kiss-of-life giving
I will second chance restore
Just hold my hand
And take a walk along my river

Uncertain

I was shocked and disbelieving
When you spoke to me
It was not like you whispered
Not like you crept into my bedroom at dawn and slowly roused
    me from sleep
You laughed and danced and shouted and skipped
Into my vision
You found me amusing
I challenged your very existence
Your right to reality
Well, can you blame me?
I was happy tucked up in abstract philosophy
Am happy with the concept of never, forever and always still
But you told me to doubt my own reality
You used my abstract against me
And should I find myself in existence
I should accept the possibilities
Being offered to me
I guess we should always accept the possibility of being wrong
Or right
Or unsure anymore
Well if you keep talking
I will have to keep listening

Hope
(For Mark)

I wanted to wake up in your arms
But I stole away under the soft moon
I wanted to lay and just hold you while you slept
But I was pulled away too soon
I wanted to listen to you breathing
I wanted to hear you speak
Of dreams yet unfulfilled
Of a life that could be better
Of a world that could be peaceful
Of me, and that I could be happy
If I could
I would
Go back
And kiss you before you kissed me
And although I know it can't be
It was simple reality that made me
Happy

Unconscious Creativity

There is a divine comedy within creation
That encourages us to let go
Not to take ourselves too seriously
To simply go with the flow
For every time I raise my pen
And battle with the page
I demand my own creativity
Only to find I have nothing to say
But in the wee hours of darkness
When I am too tired to fight
Inspiration sneaks upon me
Fills my eyes with light
Blindly I stumble forth
All physical form left behind
And I see all the methods of
Painting between the lies
I hide a message of remembrance
Within every stroke of fate
To remind myself of divine
When hungry and paint covered, I awake...

Late

I heard my name
When you called me again today
But I am forever the rabbit late
And I merely ran away
It wasn't until I stopped
And heard no sound upon the breeze
That I realised if I stopped listening
You would stop calling to me

Listening

She smiles at me
And in her eye I see
All the things she would say to me
If she but only had the words
Then again I am aware
Whenever I feel her near
That it is I who needs to hear
The stories I never heard
I raise my eyes
And seek her sight
And bathe within her soft light
To ease my troubled soul
I wax and wane
She does the same
And together we play the game
Of phases to become whole

Beyond Tomorrow

Within the fire we all become
Ancient man mesmerised
The simple tasks tire the hands
The good life, a hard life
There is no more bartering
Haggling, begging and coaxing
We are beyond the desire for more
No more hoping
Within the water we all become
The reason for living and loving
The fetch water carry wood
A philosophy of having
There is no more waterfall
Overspill, cascade of emotion
We are beyond the stagnant
Carried away in tidal motion
Within the earth we all become
A nurtured plant with face
Lifted towards the sun
Moving in place
There is no more receiving
Merely sowing and reaping
We are beyond the taking
Storing and heaping
Within the wind we all become
The cry of voices unleashed and free
The wind removes the wool from our eyes
And finally we can see
There is no more forgiving
No more ifs, buts, I wish, I need
We are beyond the arguments

It simply is, and we simply be

With

With the fire we burn to survive
With water we respect our lives
With earth we learn a new way
With the wind we sing a new day

This Light

I sit within the spotlight
The stage in darkness lies
Preparing to perform
The arts of times gone by
The light washes down
Upon my upturned face
My tools about me shine
Blessed by unearthly grace
Within the shadows I hear
Soft anticipating sighs
Waiting for my hands to move
And open up all eyes
And I feel blessed
Refreshed
And inspired to be
I craft
And bend
And prophesy
I spin
And weave
All manner of life
I bend
And blend
The Craft of the Wise
For this light is the perfect time
The blending of body and mind
A chance for us all to divine

Woven

Grandmother spider
Weave me a new web
One I can throw around me
Like a comfort
Cover it in morning dew
Let it sparkle in the sunlight
Let me tangle myself up in my dreams
Attract it all towards me
Fragile and strong
A lifetime long
And only a second of connection

Rose Petals

I fell to the earth
Upon roses made of thorns
Through the cloying fragrance and clawing dance
I learned to stand barefoot
And count every star in the sky
I stood under infinity
For but a second it seemed
And then I heard a song
It sang of love, loss, bittersweet razorblades of wisdom
It tasted salty to my tongue
Cold to my skin
Dry to my throat
But I breathed in every note
Until the razorblades heated molten through my bones
I jumped, skipped, stamped, clapped
And became the heart beat, drum beat
Violent and unafraid
Blazing, brazen, bold and brave
Frenzied I called out to the icy stars, the hare in the Moon
And stared down the Sun
Until my throat was sore
My eyes red raw
And my skin cracked under the intense heat
Then the tears of freedom became more than a release
Water to cleanse
Purify
Protect within the womb
Wash out the infected wound
Clear the air and nurture the growing life around us
I was dirty, sunburnt, sore, wrung out, wretched, wet and unable
    to speak

I was no longer afraid
I wrung out my hair and it smelt of rose petals

My Faith

As I sit here
Surrounded by soft light
This could be any day
Somewhen and never
Somewhere and nowhere
I smile into the stillness
And know that love and life revolves around this –
The moments of No Time and No Space
The hour long seconds of simple appreciation,
And I understand so little and yet so much,
For to know that we know so little makes us the wisest of all.
Little moments of clarity,
This is my faith
This is my belief
These precious seconds before life comes bustling back in.

About the Author

Romany Rivers is a wife, a sleep deprived mama, a human servant to a very mischievous cat, an artist, a Reiki Master and a Pagan High Priestess. British born and bred, Romany and her husband moved from the south of England to beautiful Nova Scotia, Canada, to pursue their dreams of a more sustainable, family focussed and rural lifestyle.

Romany has used writing, and in particular poetry, to make sense of the world around her from a very young age. As a Priestess and co-founder of Moon River Wicca, she has used poetry and modern interpretations of fairy tales in celebrations, festivals, and rituals to weave a lyrical melody into structured formats. Aside from her work as a Priestess, Artist and Author, she is also well known for her work in the holistic health community as a Reiki Master and Tarot Reader. Romany currently enjoys turning her hand to various arts and crafts; gardening and growing her own food; and watching her children discover the wondrous world around them.

This is Romany's first published anthology of poetry. This selection covers a very personal journey through the years overcoming severe bouts of depression and consequently creating a more holistic lifestyle. The chapters *Red Letters*, *Return to Sender* and *Addressee Unknown* chronicle periods of depression and anxiety; anger and healing; and acceptance and spiritual growth. All of these poems are personal in nature, but Romany believes that now is the time to share them with others. She hopes that the reader can find a connection with them, be that through empathy or understanding for themselves or for loved ones.

"Every journey is unique, but occasionally we find ourselves walking in each other's footsteps."

Romany

Moon Books invites you to begin or deepen your encounter with Paganism, in all its rich, creative, flourishing forms.